Volume V

Bock's Best

Note: Those titles marked (*) are brand new arrangements and do not appear in any other Fred Bock piano collection.

FRED'S FOREWORD

OLD FRIENDS AND NEW FRIENDS

In his new song, *Old Friends*, our friend Bill Gaither tells about the richness of long-term friendships. He is right; there *is* something comforting, comfortable, and just plain wonderful about being with old friends. Our history with Bill and Gloria goes way back. Our mutual friends, Bob and Joy MacKenzie introduced us about thirty years ago, and together we've been co-writers, business partners, fellow music publishers, have raised our kids together, and spent wonderful vacations together on Nantucket Island. We feel comfortable, comforted, and just plain wonderful spending time with old friends. My wife, Lois, and I have several friends we've not seen for years, but when we *do* see them it's like we've never been apart: we just pick up where we left off. That's the great part of "old friends".

The old friend that goes back the farthest with me is Ira. He and I were good buddies back in 8th grade, at P.S. 170 in Jamaica, New York. Ira and I used to set up the movie projector in the school auditorium. When we graduated, we each went our separate ways, but a few years ago I happened to think of Ira and decided to give him a phone call. I admit I was shocked when the information operator actually had a listing for him still living in the same area of New York City where we had grown up many moons ago. I called him (he did remember who I was) and we got together for dinner and a long visit recalling the names of our 8th grade classmates. As I remember it, the restaurant owner finally had to ask us to leave so he could lock up and go home! Ira and I have seen each other a few times since our big New York reunion. I like being with him: he's part of my history. Thanks, Ira, for being my old friend. About now, many might now be asking, "So what does your 'trip down memory lane' have to do with this new piano book?" Watch how I masterfully weave these thoughts together.

As I see it, the uniqueness of my piano writing has always been those rich, unusual harmonic progressions. "Hot chords" some might say. Well, yes, but I want them to be chords that fit comfortably into the context of the musical arrangement I've created. Some of these chords were brand new friends back in Volumes 1,2,3 and 4 of this *Bock's Best* series. But by now, some have been used again and again, and have become part of my musical vocabulary....let's call them old friends, if you will. When I sit myself down at the piano to write these arrangements, (every note by hand...none of that play-it-into-the-computer stuff for me!) I call on some of my old chord friends to help me create something interesting. Occasionally, I stumble onto a new friend: a chord I've not used before. Of course this new friend will never take the place of my tried and true old-chord friends....or will it? Before too long, I notice some of my new friends have become old friends. And that's really the point of this message. Keep your old friends (personally and musically) but keep adding new friends. And then introduce those new friends to your old friends. If you'll look across the page, I'll introduce you to some new friends you'll find in this book:

A recent photo of Mr. Bock, taken last Summer while he was working on new arrangements for this book. Note unorthodox finger positioning: a decided plus for playing his music. [Photo by Mommy Bock]

Found on page ______

NOTE: As you find your new friends, list their current address in the space indicated.

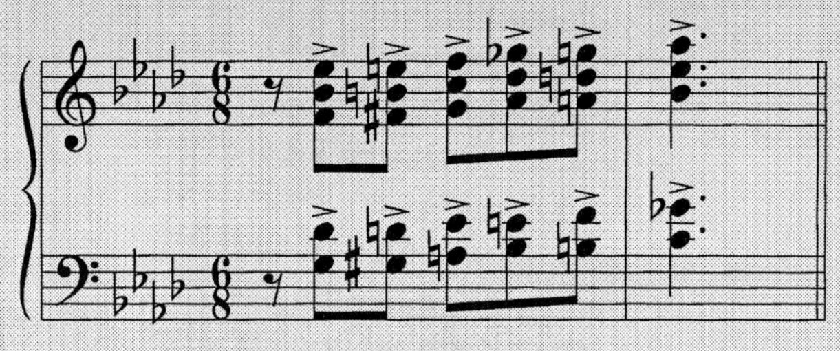

Found on page ______

Found on page ______

Found on page ______

Found on page ______

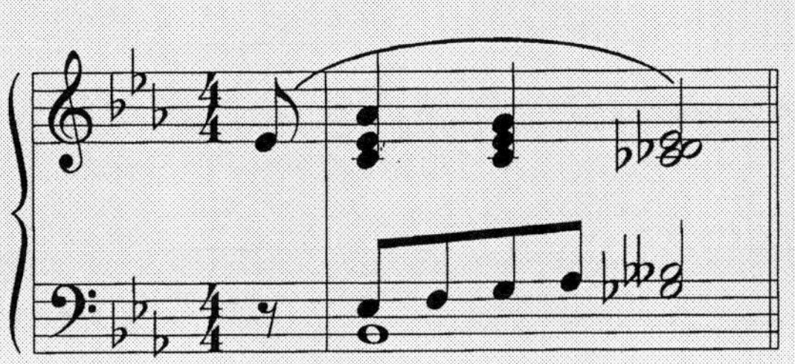

Found on page ______

Found on page ______

Found on page ______

Found on page ______

Found on page ______

Found on page ______

Found on page ______

Found on page ______

Found on page ______

These music samples were carefully engraved by my good and *old friend*, Dick Bolks.

COMPLETE LISTING OF BOCK'S BEST PIANO ARRANGEMENTS

PASS IT ON

Kurt Kaiser
Arranged by Fred Bock

Gently (♩ =±92)

mp
mf
f

a little faster
mf
ten.
ten.
a tempo
f
f

ON EAGLE'S WINGS

Michael Joncas

Arranged by Fred Bock

With affirmation (♩ =84)

ten.
f
ten.
mp
mf
mf
f
a little brighter
1

p
f
mf
mf
f
mp
mf
rit.
r.h.

THE MAJESTY AND GLORY OF YOUR NAME

Tom Fettke
Adapted by Fred Bock

With awe and mystery (♩=88)

mf
mp
p
l.h.
8va
mf
subito
p
mp

f
subito
p
f
tenderly
mp
slight accellerando
rit.

slight ritard
f
slight accellerando
ff
subito p
f
ff
mf
8va
pp
p
pp
l.h.

OPEN OUR EYES

Bob Cull
Arranged by Fred Bock

ppp
let fade away

HOLY GROUND

Geron Davis
Arranged by Fred Bock

a little faster
mf
f
f
mf
mp
p

WE GATHER TOGETHER

Netherlands Folk Hymn
Arranged by Fred Bock

mp
mp
mf

f
mp
mel.
mf
mel.
mf
legato
mp
mf
8va (both hands)
f
rit.
l.h.
ff

WONDERFUL GRACE OF JESUS

Haldor Lillenas
Arranged by Fred Bock

mp
melody
mf
f

3
r.h.
gliss on
black notes in rhythm
ff as fast as you can play
8va
fff
8ba

OUR GOD REIGNS

Leonard E. Smith, Jr.
Arranged by Fred Bock

mf
f
r.h.
f

ff
ad lib.
l.h.
ff

WE BRING THE SACRIFICE OF PRAISE

Kirk Dearman
Arranged by Fred Bock

mf
l.h.
ff
legato
mf
ff
legato
mf
ff
l.h.
legato
mf

legato
ff
mf
mf
f
ff
r.h.
fff
8ba

I WALKED TODAY WHERE JESUS WALKED

Geoffrey O'Hara
Arranged by Fred Bock

Warmly and tenderly (♩=92)

mp
mf

3
ten.
3
ten.
mp
mp
mf
mel.

bring out melody notes
ff
mp
rit.
ten.

HOW EXCELLENT IS THY NAME

Dick & Melodie Tunney and Paul Smith
Arranged by Fred Bock

Brightly, with energy and rhythmic drive (♩ =120)

1.
2.
f
Furioso
rit.
ff
fff

GRACE GREATER THAN OUR SIN

(Marvelous Grace)

Daniel B. Towner

Arranged by Fred Bock

f
rit.
subito
p
mp

VICTORY IN JESUS

Eugene M. Bartlett, Sr.
Arranged by Fred Bock

Strongly, with energy (♩=100)

a bit slower

mp
ff
8va
8va

I'LL FLY AWAY

Albert E. Brumly
Arranged by Fred Bock

Bright and happy (♩=120)

legato
legato
mf
l.h.

7
7
f
ff
(both hands)
8va
15ma
ff
ff
(both hands)
15ma
ff
l.h.

HE IS LORD

Traditional
Arranged by Fred Bock

rit.
Strongly
f
mf
f
mp
ten.
ten.
ten.
mf
ten.
ten.
ten.
f
r.h.
l.h.
subito
p
mf
mf
f

IN THE GARDEN

C. Austin Miles
Arranged by Fred Bock

In a meditative style (♩ =92)

ten.
ten.
slight rit.
a tempo
(♭)
f
mf
mf
f
4/4
mf
ten.
ten.
ten.
8va
mp

JESUS, NAME ABOVE ALL NAMES

Naida Hearn
Arranged by Fred Bock

a tempo
(b)
(rit. 2x)
(optional repeat)
a tempo
9
8
ten. ten. ten.
mp
ten. ten. ten.

HE IS EXALTED

Twila Paris
Arranged by Fred Bock

With exuberance and rhythmic drive

1.
2.
mf
mf

8va (both hands)
8va

HAVE THINE OWN WAY, LORD

George C. Stebbins
Arranged by Fred Bock

In a broad, flowing style (♩. =58)

rit.
mf

WHAT A MIGHTY GOD WE SERVE

Traditional
Arranged by Fred Bock

8va
f
p
(like an echo)
f

*"A Mighty Fortress Is Our God"

I WONDER AS I WANDER

Collected by John Jacob Niles
Arranged by Fred Bock

Tenderly and wistfully (♩=72)

mf
f
both hands
8va
mp
mf
f
8va
ten.

ten.
ten.
mf
ten.
mp
mf
f
both hands
8va
ten.
mf
both hands
8va
mf

HYMN OF PROMISE

Natalie Sleeth
Arranged by Fred Bock

Moderato (♩=80)

mf
mp
mf
mp
mf
no ritard!
mf

WHEN THE ROLL IS CALLED UP YONDER

James M. Black
Arranged by Fred Bock

f
3
mp
f
legato
ff
mf

Light blues feel (♩. =±60)
ten.
mp
12
8
mf
f
mf

f
mf
no decrescendo!
mf

MORNING HAS BROKEN

English Folktune
Arranged by Fred Bock

Moderato (almost one beat to the bar) (♩ =120)

f
mf

mf
f

AS THE DEER

Marty Nystrom
Arranged by Fred Bock

a tempo
p
mp
mf
f
mp
mf
f

strongly
slight
rit.
mf
l.h.
f
mf
mp
mp
r.h.
p

LORD, BE GLORIFIED/SANCTUARY

Bob Kilpatrick
John Thompson & Randy Scruggs
Arranged by Fred Bock

rit.
mf

With a Gospel feel (♩ = 72)
"Sanctuary"
light rhythm

Stronger, more driving
f
suddenly slowing
mf
(♩ = 60)
mp
ten.
mf
ten.
mp
8va
pp
8ba
pp

THIS IS THE DAY

Les Garrett
Arranged by Fred Bock

mf
(echo)
mp
simile
mf
(echo)
mp
mf
like a fanfare
mf
f
3
mf legato
3

(echo)
mp
mf
(echo)
mp
mf
scherzo-like
no pedal!
f
l.h.
legato
mf
legato
f
OK to pedal now!
mf
f
8va
ff
l.h.
(ff)
r.h.

TURN YOUR EYES UPON JESUS

Helen Lemmel
Arranged by Fred Bock

Warmly (♩=92)

f
firmly
warmly
mf
mp
mf

relaxed tempo
ff
mf
slight rit.
ten.
ten.
ten.
mf
slight accellerando
a tempo
mp
accellerando
8va
mp
rit.
r.h.
p

HE HAS MADE ME GLAD

Leona Von Brethorst
Arranged by Fred Bock

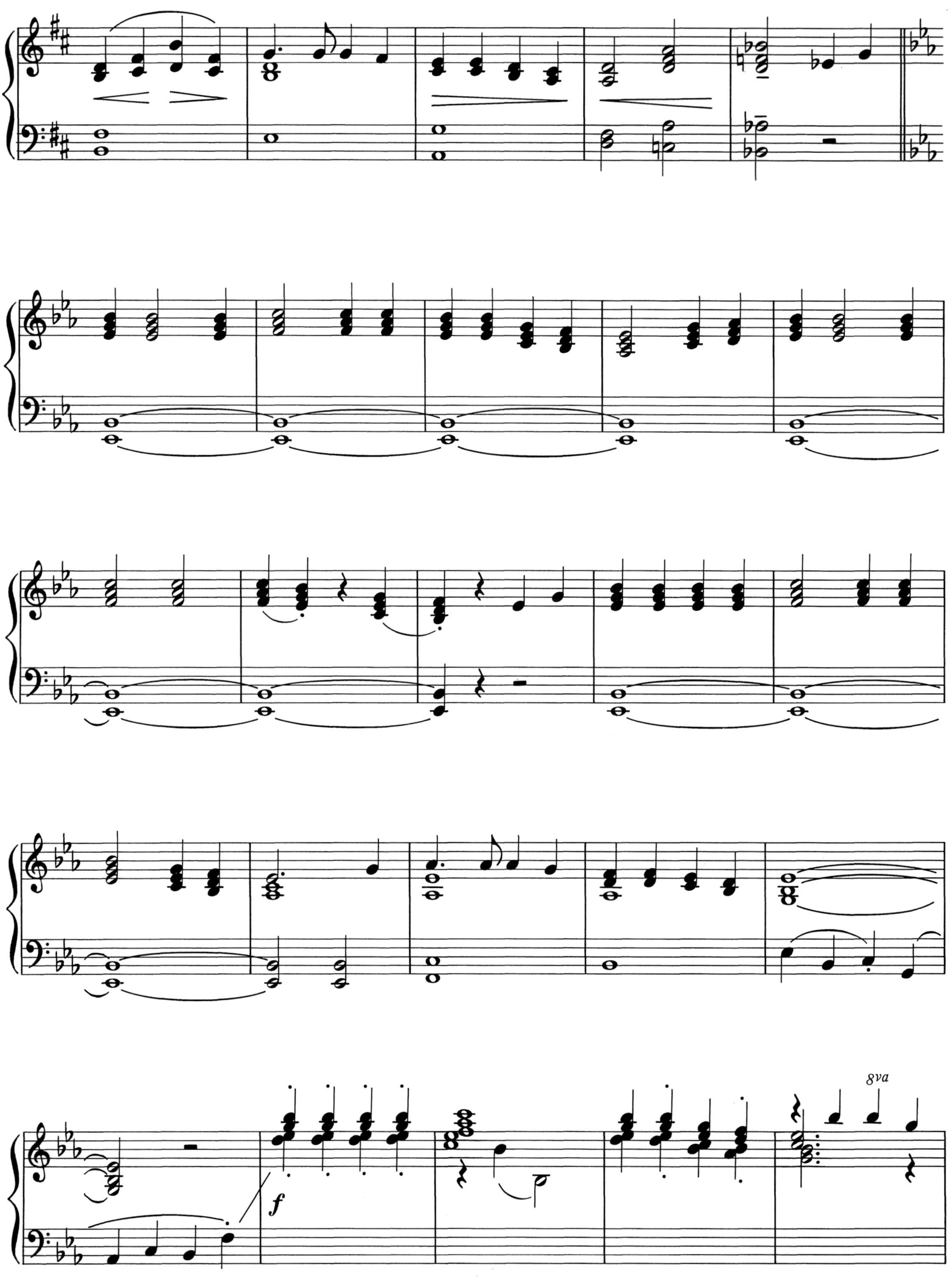
f
8va

8va
8va
f
8va
ff
no ritard!
mf
both hands 8va
ff
mf

OLD FRIENDS

William J. Gaither & J.D. Miller
Arranged by Fred Bock

In a relaxed, easy tempo (♩ =80)

mp
mf
f
8va
mf

HERE I AM, LORD

Dan Schutte
Arranged by Fred Bock

f
mf
ten.
mp
ten.

f
ff
f
mf
smoothly

f
f
accellerendo
l.h.
f
rit.
mf

GLORIFY THY NAME

Donna Adkins
Arranged by Fred Bock

mp like a hymn
mf
p
mp
mf
f
mf
f
ff
mp
8va (both hands)

A BALM IN GILEAD

Traditional Spiritual
Arranged by Fred Bock

a little brighter
mf
f
r.h.
l.h.

mp
mel.
sub.
p
ten.
mf
mp
rit.
mp

HALLE, HALLE, HALLE

Traditional Caribbean
Arranged by Fred Bock

brightly
legato
mf
f
brightly
legato
r.h. legato
subito
p
f

accellerando
Broaden
ff
rit.
brightly
(both hands)
8va
r.h.
l.h.
ff

BE THOU MY VISION

Irish Folk Melody
Arranged by Fred Bock

ten.
ten.
Ped.

PRAISE THE NAME OF JESUS

Roy Hicks, Jr.
Arranged by Fred Bock

mf
bring out l.h. melody
mp
mf
mf
f
mp
mf
mf

mf
Stately
mf
f
gradual rit.
mf
p

THE LORD'S PRAYER

Albert Hay Mallotte
Arranged by Fred Bock

8ba
p dolce
r.h.
l.h.
mf
mf

(echo)
p
mf
ten.
strongly (bring out melody notes)
f
ff
fff
mf
mp
pp
r.h.

AWESOME GOD/I EXALT THEE

Richard Mullins
Pete Sanchez, Jr.
Arranged by Fred Bock

* play with side of thumb.

mf

mp
rit.
pp

THE LOVE OF GOD

Frederick H. Lehman
Arranged by Fred Bock

With great expression and warmth (♩=80)

ten.
ten.
f
ff
a tempo
slight rit.
(ff)

SHINE, JESUS, SHINE

Graham Kendrick
Arranged by Fred Bock

slight rit.
a tempo
legato
a tempo
f
f

both hands 8va
loco
ten.
(like a harp)
rit.
sub.
ten.
warm and legato

sub.
rit.
a tempo
(like the beginning)
8va
ten.
a tempo
loco
ten.
slight rit.
8va
8va

GOD SO LOVED THE WORLD

John Stainer
Arranged by Fred Bock

mp
mp
mp

rit.
f

p
ten.
ten.
pp

SING HALLELUJAH TO THE LORD

Linda Stassen
Arranged by Fred Bock

slower
a tempo
f
slowing
a tempo
both hand 8va
mp
f
mf

I WILL CALL UPON THE LORD

Michael O'Shields
Arranged by Fred Bock

f
mf
f
mf

f
mf
8va
l.h.
8ba

JUST AS I AM

William B. Bradbury
Arranged by Fred Bock

Tenderly (♩ =80)

a little faster
slowing

a tempo
l.h.
mf
mp
r.h.
p
8ba

GESU BAMBINO

Pietro A. Yon
Arranged by Fred Bock

(♩.=52)
a little brighter
ten. ten.
mf

pp
play lower note in r.h. stronger than top note
mp
mf
legato
ten.
2
2
2
2
ten.
(♭)
ten.
ten.

mf
mf
p slower
pp
very slowly and deliberate
both hands
8va
pp
ppp

I SURRENDER ALL

Winfield S. Weeden
Arranged by Fred Bock

ff
f
mp
poco accellerando
mf
f
rit.
mp
mf
ten.
ten.
p
pp
Ped.

ALL HAIL, KING JESUS

Dave Moody
Arranged by Fred Bock

f
f
mf
3
melody legato
ten.
3
f

allargando
ff
slight accellerando
f
ff broaden
ff
grandioso
l.h.
r.h.
both hands 8va
fff

EMMANUEL

Bob McGee
Arranged by Fred Bock

With awe and mystery (𝅗𝅥 = 60)

* "O Come, O Come, Emmanuel"
Traditional Plainsong Chant

(♭)
(♮)
1
(♭)
(♭)
f
(♭)
l.h.
l.h.
both hands 8va
p

Will there be a

Bock's Best

#6?